PEOPLE IN HISTORY

Guy Fawkes

Stephen White-Thomson

WAYLAND

Explore the world with **Popcorn** - your complete first non-fiction library.

Look out for more titles in the Popcorn range. All books have the same format of simple text and striking images. Text is carefully matched to the pictures to help readers to identify and understand key vocabulary. www.waylandbooks.co.uk/popcorn

First published in 2013 by Wayland
Copyright © Wayland 2013

Wayland
Hachette Children's Books
338 Euston Road
London NW1 3BH

Wayland Australia
Level 17/207 Kent Street
Sydney NSW 2000

Produced for Wayland by
White-Thomson Publishing Ltd
www.wtpub.co.uk
+44 (0)843 208 7460

Editor: Stephen White-Thomson
Designer: Clare Nicholas
Picture researcher: Stephen White-Thomson
Series consultant: Kate Ruttle
Design concept: Paul Cherrill

A catalogue for this title is available from the British Library

941'.061'092-dc23

978 0 7502 7916 1

10 9 8 7 6 5 4 3 2 1

Wayland is a division of Hachette Children's Books,
an Hachette UK company.
www.hachette.co.uk

Printed and bound in China

Picture/illustration credits:
Bridgeman Art Library: 8, 9, 18, 16, 17 Look and Learn;
Peter Bull 23; Getty: cover, 11, 12, 16; Shutterstock:
Dmitry Naumov 19, Bikeworldtravel 2/21; Wikimedia:
4, 5, 12.

Every effort has been made to clear copyright.
Should there be any inadvertent omission,
please apply to the publisher for rectification.

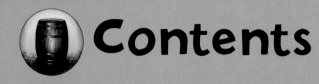 Contents

Guy Fawkes' England

Guy Fawkes was born in April 1570 when Queen Elizabeth I was queen of England. She was a Protestant. Some English people were Catholics. They were treated badly.

Elizabeth I was queen of England for 45 years, from 1558 to 1603.

Elizabeth I died in 1603 and the Protestant James I became king. He was unkind to Catholics, too. Guy Fawkes wanted to kill him.

This is King James I. Guy is famous for trying to blow him up in the Gunpowder Plot.

Early life

Guy's family lived in York. His father was called Edward. His mother's name was Edith. He had two sisters, Anne and Elizabeth. His father was a Protestant.

Guy plays marbles with his friends.

When Guy was eight, his father died. Edith married a Catholic called Denis. Guy became a Catholic. Many of his family's friends were also Catholic.

This Catholic family had to keep their religion a secret.

Going to school

Guy went to St. Peter's School in York.
Schools were very strict then! Jack and
Kit Wright went to the same school.
They were both in the Gunpowder Plot.

A child is getting beaten in the corner for misbehaving!

Schools were mainly for rich boys. Only a few girls went to school. Students used hornbooks to learn the alphabet and numbers.

Guy probably used a hornbook like this one.

In summer, school started at six in the morning and finished at five in the afternoon!

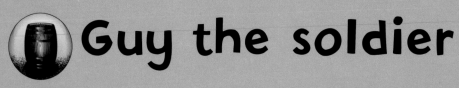 Guy the soldier

Around 1593, Guy left England and
became a soldier in the Spanish army.
Guy was good at fighting
and learned how to
use gunpowder.

Guy changed
his name to
Guido, which
is Spanish
for Guy.

This is the uniform that
Guy wore as a soldier.

The Spanish were Catholics. Guy wanted them to attack England and get rid of the Protestant King, James I. They did not want to help.

This is how Guy looked at the time of the Gunpowder Plot.

The plotters

Since Spain wouldn't help, some English Catholics made their own plan to kill the king. Robert Catesby was their leader.

This picture shows some of the plotters together.

Catesby asked Guy to join the plot. The other main plotters were Thomas Winter, Thomas Percy, and Jack Wright.

The plotters promised to keep the Gunpowder Plot a secret.

13

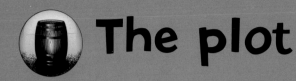

The plot

Their plot was to blow up King James I, his wife and his elder son in the Houses of Parliament. They also wanted to kill lots of other important people.

This is what the Houses of Parliament looked like in 1605.

In the Spring of 1605, the plotters rented a cellar under the Houses of Parliament. Guy Fawkes hid 36 barrels of gunpowder in the cellar.

Guy was ready to light the gunpowder at the right time.

Discovered!

One of the plotters wrote to his relative, Lord Monteagle. He told him not to go to Parliament on 5 November. King James heard about the plot.

This is the lantern that Guy used to light up the dark cellar.

Very early in the morning of
5 November, James's soldiers found
Guy in the cellar with the barrels
of gunpowder. They arrested him.

Guy is caught by James's men next to the gunpowder.

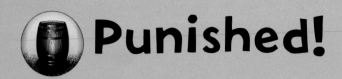

Punished!

When the plot was discovered, Catesby and others escaped to the country. They were caught and killed.

Catesby was the leader of the plotters.

The same bullet killed Catesby and Percy.

Guy Fawkes was kept in the Tower of London. He was tortured. Then he was executed in January 1606 with some of the other plotters.

Guy Fawkes Night

On 5 November 1605, Londoners lit
bonfires to celebrate King James I's
escape from death. More than 400
years later, we are still celebrating!

This rhyme is about the Gunpowder Plot.

Remember, remember, the fifth of November,

Gunpowder, Treason and Plot,

We know no reason why Gunpowder Treason

Should ever be forgot.

Every year, on 5 November, we build big bonfires. We sometimes burn a guy on the bonfire. We send fireworks shooting up into the sky.

Fireworks explode above the Houses of Parliament in London.

21

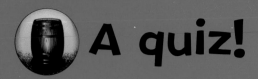 # A quiz!

Read through the book again and see if you can answer these questions!

1. The Gunpowder Plot was an attempt to kill whom?
   a. Elizabeth I
   b. James I
   c. Henry VIII

2. Who was the leader of the Gunpowder Plot?
   a. Robert Catesby
   b. Thomas Winter
   c. Guy Fawkes

3. In which year did the Gunpowder Plot happen?
   a. 1600
   b. 1610
   c. 1605

4. How many barrels of gunpowder were found in the cellars?
   a. 25
   b. 36
   c. 48

Make a Guy Fawkes hat

You will need:
- black card for hat
- silver card for buckle
- coloured paper for feather
- scissors • glue

If you make this hat, you can wear it and look like Guy Fawkes. Or you can put it on a 'guy' for Guy Fawkes Night!

1. Roll a piece of black card around your head into a tube shape. Glue the two edges together. Draw round the top of the tube to create a circle for the top of your hat. Cut the circle out.

2. Cut eight small strips of black card, then fold the strips in half. Use the strips to attach the circle to the top of the tube.

3. Cut out a large circle for the rim of your hat. Place the tube in the middle of the circle and draw round it. Cut out the small circle, so that the rim can sit on your head. Use 8 more strips of card to attach the rim to the tube. Decorate with buckle and feather.

Glossary

arrested when people arrest someone, they take them prisoner

bonfire a large fire that you make outside

Catholics people who believe that the pope is the head of their religion

executed to have your head cut off

firework something that explodes with coloured lights and loud bangs

gunpowder a powder that easily explodes when it is set alight

hornbook something that children held in their hands to help them learn the alphabet and simple numbers

Houses of Parliament the buildings where the people who make British laws meet

lantern a candle inside a container

plot a secret plan

Protestant people who believe that the king or queen is the head of their religion

religion a religion is a set of ideas that people have about a god or gods

torture to hurt or punish someone, often to find out information

treason a crime against a country or its king or queen

Index

EXPLORE THE WORLD WITH THE POPCORN NON-FICTION LIBRARY!

- Develops children's knowledge and understanding of the world by covering a wide range of topics in a fun, colourful and engaging way
- Simple sentence structure builds readers' confidence
- Text checked by an experienced literacy consultant and primary deputy-head teacher
- Closely matched pictures and text enable children to decode words
- Includes a cross-curricular activity in the back of each book

FREE DOWNLOADS!

OVER 50 TITLES TO CHOOSE FROM!

- Written by an experienced teacher
- Learning objectives clearly marked
- Provides information on where the books fit into the curriculum
- Photocopiable so pupils can take them home

www.waylandbooks.co.uk/downloads